HOLD THE RAIN
IN YOUR HANDS

Poems New and Selected

HOLD THE RAIN IN YOUR HANDS

Poems New and Selected

GLEN SORESTAD

COTEAU BOOKS

Most of the new work in this book has appeared, or will appear, often in earlier versions, in the following publications: *Aurora 1979* (Doubleday), *Descant, Nebula Alpha, NeWest Review, Quarry, Cross-Canada Writers' Quarterly, Dandelion, Poetry Canada Review, Kunapipi* (Denmark), *Canadian Literature, Prism International, Pierian Spring, Arc, Canadian Author and Bookman*, also in the anthology *100% Cracked Wheat*, in *Canadian Literature 100*, and *Prism International's* 25th anniversary anthology. Many of the poems have been broadcast on CBC radio, either on "Anthology" or "Ambience".

Cover illustration by Wilf Perreault
Courtesy of Woltjen/Udell Gallery, Edmonton
Design by Carolyn Deby
Photograph by Alex Campbell
Produced by Centax of Canada
Printed by Hignell Printing Ltd.

The author wishes to acknowledge the editorial insights of Patrick Lane in the selection and arrangement of the poems, as well as for his advice and assistance in the revisions of some of the new work.

We gratefully acknowledge the assistance of the Saskatchewan Arts Board and the Canada Council in the publication of this book.

 Saskatchewan
Arts Board

Canadian Cataloguing in Publication Data

Sorestad, Glen A., 1937-
    Hold the rain in your hands

ISBN 0-919926-41-X (bound). — ISBN 0-919926-40-1 (pbk.)

I. Title.
PS8587.0746H64 1985   C811'.54   C85-091080-3
PR9199.3.S67H64 1985

coteau books

Thunder Creek Publishing Co-operative Limited
Box 239, Substation #1
Moose Jaw, Saskatchewan
S6H 5V0

C O N T E N T S

from PEAR SEEDS IN MY MOUTH

from WIND SONGS

from PRAIRIE PUB POEMS

C O N T E N T S

NEW POEMS

Poem for Sonia

I would never write another poem
if only I could show you
in a few perfect lines
what the touch of your fingers
on my aging cheek
means

Just a Kid in Vancouver

Just a kid in Vancouver
    pulling a wagonload of dreams
        down East Broadway,
    tossing spiny-coated chestnuts
        at passing streetcars,
    retrieving pancaked pennies
        after the streetcar passed.

The kid wheeled his wagon
    down gravelled alleys screaming
        off to his latest four-alarm fire,
    scaring the Japanese fish-peddlers
        plying their back-alley salmon,
or sometimes he clanked down sidewalks
    a victorious tank rumbling from the war
        just over but not forgotten,
occasionally a four-wheeled fruit truck
    leaving the neighbour's apple tree,
        one-legging away his booty.

The kid in Vancouver is gone now,
as is the tousled farm boy he became.
Only in the sporadic dreams of a sleeper
is there still a kid in Vancouver
    pulling a wagonload of dreams
        down East Broadway.

McGillivray's Pear Tree — 1944

A pear tree grew in Tom McGillivray's yard,
a tree from which we kids were not allowed
to pick — not one experimental bite.
We could pick apples, cherries, any fruit,
but not the fruit from this enchanted tree:
for so it was for us, unknowing of
society's strange dictates and demands.

Then one dark night while old McGillivray slept,
unlearned in the letters of the night,
I slipped into his yard. Beneath that tree,
uncertain of what perils might befall,
I tasted the forbidden pear; the taste
confirmed my going out that quiet night.
Since then I've lived with pear seeds in my mouth.

Wasyl Fofonoff

At a hundred, old Wasyl Fofonoff
could still pound fence posts
just as he had always done
since he claimed his land
near Buchanan village
after the century's turn,
leaving Russia before Lenin
and the scourge of Stalin,
taking up the great migration
of Doukhobors to a new land.

By one hundred and ten
he still rode the mower
in the hayfield
on a hot July day
while his neighbours,
sweating and miserable
under the sun blast,
were ready to bet
Wasyl would outlive them all,
maybe live forever.
Even the young woman
who'd married him when
he was only seventy or so
was no longer a young woman
and had given up any notion
of actually surviving him.

At a hundred fifteen, Wasyl,
what strange ghosts haunt your dreams?

Are you drawn back to Russia,
another century, another world?

What sleek young darkeyed
peasant girl dances
through hundred year old dreams
of an ancient Russian farmer
who has outlived his own children,
his lovers and his enemies,
has seen the earth swallow them
while he, outcast, lives on
in a world of ghosts
and vague dreams from another century?

Puberty Rite: Saskatchewan, Circa 1952

First date:
sitting in the backseat of a '49 Chev
with a big-breasted Polish girl
two years older
a hundred years more experienced
saying things
that she would somehow manage to finish
trying to recall
what all those paperback lovers said
failing to remember.

After the movie:
driving back home
night now a blessing
to conceal the awkwardness
the indecision, the hopeless inadequacy
babbling about the movie
until she has to stop your lips
with hers
guide your clumsy sweaty hands
with hers
and you tremble
with a perfect joy
that can never
be equalled.

The next day:
you believe your voice is deeper
more manly, more mature
and you wonder if anyone around
will notice the difference.

For a Retired English Professor

Thirty-six years of teaching English
and now in the monotony
of forced retirement
he shows the pain of
the withdrawal symptoms
as he reads the letters
from his sons and daughters
in his book-cluttered study
with red marking pen in hand.

Remembrance Day Program

It is a day like any other day:
a sweaty classroom struggling
with a pageful of abstracts
eyes flickering occasionally
from notebooks to clock
above the front chalkboard.

The low mixed hum of work and shirk
fractures again with the metallic intrusion
of the intercom. It is eleven a.m.

>*Attention Please! Mr. Blatt*
>*will now give the Remembrance*
>*Day address to be followed by*
>*the traditional two minute*
>*silence . . .*

(a condition foreign to most places
where things happen)

After the clichés come the remembrances:

>*We will now stand and observe*
>*two minutes silence to remember.*

The students remain seated. The room
is choked for two minutes in an awkward
silence;

except for the intercom which continues
its electric nonsilence, emitting
reminders of its omniscience:
the rattling of paper as the speaker
still stands by the live mike
with expended speech clutched in fist
his heavy breathing filling the intercom
with life and the classroom
with a constant reminder:

it is easier to contemplate now and tomorrow
than to reflect on death in 1917 or 1942.

The second hand sweeps the attack
of silence through two slow revolutions
and each one is left to his own thoughts
in silence.

    Thank you. That is all.

The intercom completes its usual fadeaway
and the classroom hum is restored to life.
The clock says 11:08.

The teacher returns to unmarked papers;
the students resume their clockwatching
with mock-industrious expressions.
The classroom struggles on again;
it is a day like any other day.

Poem in a Restaurant

If I could have written a poem
on the back of a dollar-laden conversation
I would have.

When you walked in
the silver on my tongue
turned to lead,
your eyes burned
across the years between us.

I failed then,
but I move now
across the perfect silence,
kiss your darkened eyelids
with words.

Early Morning Song

Several million electric alarms
shriek the morning to semi-life
and I thump my sleeping feet to the floor
as North America's working stiffs
thunder from bed to bathroom.

A million subdued pastel toilets
gush in one simultaneous Niagaran roar,
and when the toothbrush ritual begins
the abrasion is an infernal grating
that threatens to split my brainpan.

When I push my chair back
from my morning coffee shared alone
with my fellow millions, the scraping
of the countless chair legs echoes
in the silent house.

Hawk on a Telephone Pole

I drive by your perch slowly on the tractor.
Your eyes rotate to follow me in passing,
unblinking, without a hint of fear,
the quiet indifference of the hunter.
You are sated for the moment, at rest.
Except for the unflinching eyes
you could be merely an extension
of the lifeless telephone pole.

It is not easy to see you now,
roosted like some barnyard fowl,
the clawed killer of the sky,
dropping out of the sun
to ravage a field mouse
with terrible talons.

Except for the pent-up fury
of those slowly moving eyes
that follow me down the road —
and a long time after.

The Badger

Something in the early morning sun
that strides across the stubble
newly uncovered from winter snow
takes me somewhere
south of Wood Mountain
driving a gravel backroad
in fast waning light,
seeking the wily cock pheasant —
the day's perfect end.

But instead, the last light
captures badger, ambling unconcerned
about his shrinking world,
sunbeams splashing his silver coat
making him a miniature grizzly bear
in a world of stubble and sky.

Now, this morning, somewhere north
as sun turns last year's stubble
to the near-gold of autumn
I recall the badger,
animal of rare boyhood days,
and I wonder whether sometime
there will be another badger
somewhere to reawaken lost memories
here
in this country of growing myths.

Song for Big Bear

The tiger lilies still explode
in wild dashes of orange
forcing up through the tangle
of golden rods and brown-eyed susans,
crowded into their last stand
between grainfields and roadsteads
in this land of disappearing fences.
The wind scurries in and over
each fiery lily burst with its secrets,
with its promises and its lies.

Big Bear heard the wind at Fort Pitt;
it told him not to sign the treaty.
His horse stood patient and listened.

> the grandmother's men can not know
> what the wind says they do not know
> the cry of the wind as the last buffalo
> sank to its knees on the bloody grass
> they can not hear the wind voices
> whispering over the flaming lilies
> whispering of the people's final hunt
>
> all they hear is the shrieking
> of the iron horse on the steel
> the rattling sound of silver coins
> with the grandmother's head on them
> the white man's talk of land and ploughs

Only his people hear the wind voices
murmuring their warnings through poplars.
Big Bear heard the voices and listened,
listened with the lilies on a hill
above the twisting South Saskatchewan
where there was no barbed wire
and there were no more buffalo.

The Duck Hunters

The first wind-whispers of morning
do not ruffle the marsh where we crouch
hidden in bullrushes, answering
instincts old and grey as this dawn.

Speechless we share the silent
grip that binds us to the moment,
huddled in half-light, thigh muscles aching,
waiting in the early morning chill,

waiting for the first flocks,
the whistling wings that will drive
us into action. Our eyes and ears
probe the wakening light,

fingers wrapped on our shotguns,
locked together bone on bone,
waiting that one stimulus that will
impel us to rise as one and kill.

Red Fox in Fall

This red fox
            we have set to flight
is a flash fire
            against
the dying gold
            of the wheat stubble:

a short moment
            and we are not certain
there ever was
            a burning motion
in the fading fall
            light
that closes now
            around us.

17

Prairie Blizzard, January 1956

Morning broke mild — and deceptive,
but the cattle were not fooled.
They grew restless, milled about
with impatience as the clouds thickened,
sensing the coming storm.
The first sleet impelled them forward.

The temperature plunged, the sleet
driven by a vicious north wind
and the cattle turned south
away from the wind and the wetness
that clung and froze to their faces,
across the open rangeland they moved,
a sombre procession through
a white wilderness, away from their tormentor.

The wind rose and sleet became snow,
heavy flakes, wind-blasted against them
as they retreated, woodenly, stolidly
ever southward as in some strange trance,
their faces crusting with ice.
Down from the hill they stumbled, blinded
into the deep brush-shrouded coulee.
In the calm they rested while the wind
howled abuse overhead and the snow sifted
down to fill this gash on the open plains.

The spring air was alive with smells:
the redolence of wolf willows almost able
to dominate the stench of the herd —
their grave uncovered in the melting snow.

Old Snoozy

Eleven a.m. any morning but Sunday
the hotelkeeper at the Windsor in Buchanan
unlocks the door for old Snoozy.

Only three days as owner of the hotel,
he already knows that unlocking the door
is not the proprietorial act it seems;

he has learned in this village his hotel
can not be considered opened each morning
until Snoozy sits down with his first beer.

In the Hotel at Langham

Maybe the guy at the shuffleboard has had
too much to drink because he says,
"Have I got any more balls left?"
and looks around the bar as if expecting
someone to produce another game-piece for him.

On the next end he leans unsteadily forward
sighting eye-level down the waxed hardwood,
then proclaims to anyone who'll listen,
"I've gotta knock one-a-them assforward
and the other assbackward, know what I mean?"

It's harvest time and the bar is almost deserted
by farmers at any rate, except for this one
and his equally unsteady opponent.
"A fella's gotta know what's important.
Shuffleboard's more important than wheat!"

They finish the game and start another,
wobbling from table to game and back again.
The air outside hums with the sound of harvest.
"Should we have another? What the hell,
the old man can damn well wait."

Old Alec, Drayman

The dray horses
have given way to the truck
but old Alec still lifts
and hauls every crate and box
that keeps the town alive:
arms, shoulders and back
have hoisted several cities
in his time.

True to his forty years of draying
he never passes the hotel:
he bursts into the pub
assumes the table near the door
his table by silent right
his beer is placed before him
one bottle of Pilsener —
Alec's elixir.

He tilts it back
(no time for a glass
these forty years)
drains half the bottle
pauses
then swallows the remainder
pulls on his felt cap
and leaves.

Beer at Cochin

The lazy August fire
                wanted quenching.
Even the slightest breeze
                    from the lake
could not suppress the knowledge
that Cochin pub was near
and cool
        and wet.

Entering the dim-cool
                    (alive
with beer promises) room is
so good
        you want to stop
                        forever
the moment
        to hang suspended.

        The Indians and Métis have their own
        section in the pub at Cochin —
        no cordons
                no signs
                        no markers
        of any kind
        no, nothing so blatant.
        But in Cochin
        they know
                where to sit.
        Everyone in the room knows
                                even you
        total stranger
                even you know too.

But you ignore it and sit down
next to a table of Indians
                        and wait
and it doesn't take long
                        no
not long at all.

Someone flips a switch
                        and conversation
in the room is silenced —
and even the table next to you
is frozen.

And the bartender comes over
                        his face pained
and he asks
            if you wouldn't like to
            move closer to the bar

and you are well aware
that it isn't really a question
                        now
or ever.

Sam

The bottles and glasses
are in complete disarray
but it doesn't matter
because we are waiting
for Sam who will
rearrange the table
like a florist
before he drinks his first beer.

Acadia Valley

Acadia Valley has no pub left, just memories.
Sunburned for decades, flames ate it in hours.
The wood smoke streaked the sky, bringing men
for miles to watch the old hotel join the sun.

The rooms that no one stayed in went too,
as flames dashed upanddown the old frame:
a little wooden box of times past.
Watchers stood silent with their recollections.

Now on a hot July afternoon a thirsty farmer
drives to Alsask or Empress or Oyen.
You can drive through Acadia Valley and see
only an old dog panting in the shade.

Old Pete

It's only two in the afternoon, but already
old Pete is repeating his stories,
forgetting who has heard, who has just arrived.
The old age pension cheque he cashed yesterday
has dwindled away to another monthly memory,
a beer-soaked exchange between glass and urinal.
To the regulars of the King's Hotel it's plain
that old Pete will not last through to supper,
not that the old man ever ate much anyway.

But sometime around four o'clock old Pete
will wobble woodenly once more to the john
following the dictates of his rebellious bladder,
and lurching upright into some vestige of sense
that links the present to an earlier man,
he'll decide that he has had enough.

Bundled and belching, earflaps down
against the winter wind that sweeps the streets,
old Pete will weave unsteadily through the town,
waving at farmtrucks and familiar cars,
helloing all in sight as he totters home
to the small frame shack that houses him
and all the memories he cares to recall.

On the doorstep he stops, hesitates again,
not to search his pockets for a key though,
his doors are never locked, always secure;
but to steel his time-worn spirit,
to shore it up once more against
the silence that rushes at him.
And the emptiness within is another death.

The Climax Hotel

The hotel in Climax is signless —
nothing to identify it as a hotel
or to boast that this is Climax.
But then why should it be otherwise?

Everyone in these parts knows
perfectly well what village
this is, where the hotel is
(and always has been).

And since there isn't another
for at least ten miles around
there isn't much need
for advertising, is there?

The possibility of being
inconspicuous in Climax
seems rather remote at best.

The Pub in Alvena

The bargain store next to the hotel
is closed and so are most of the shops
along the village's main road.
We tried all the doors along the drag —
finally found two that would open.
The pool hall still survived, several tables
unoccupied, but four old men playing cards
in the back; and one general store
where the owner woke up when we opened his door
so we had to go in and buy something.

But the hotel in Alvena still thrives
though the rooms haven't seen a traveller
for years, and the pub itself couldn't hold
a decent-sized meeting of Saskatchewan's
Ku Klux Klan.

The inevitable shuffleboard dominates
the place and somehow you get the feeling
that something distinctive must have been
lost when it went in.

The tables are all occupied, except
the one nearest the door, so we slip in
crowd around it and hope we are
not assuming seats long spoken-for —
the divine right of patronage.
We decide on one beer, but change
our minds and have a second because
we have to wait so long for the first
to arrive. We have to smoke in shifts
so we can still see each other.

We shout our small talk back and forth
above the din of the Indian woman
and her uncle playing shuffleboard.
When we leave part of the smoke
and hubbub trails behind us
down the gravelled road home.

The Leader Hotel

The old farmer at the table near the door
has obviously been here
since opening time this morning
and his laughter now is spontaneous —
an explosive hiss that ejaculates
through his teeth like steam
from an antique locomotive.

The barmaid with the low-slung hips
teases the old fellow as she passes
his table with a tray of beer
makes mock-threats to phone his wife
and urge her to come to town
to take him home.

He answers her with another laugh
and launches his own series of jibes
directed at his absent and therefore
innocuous wife, concluding
"The only reason I married her
in the first place is that she
stood alongside me at the altar
with an axe."

The Commercial Hotel, Maple Creek

When you slide into a chair behind
a couple draught beers the past rises
in the foam and effervescent stories
fill your ears . . .

> the night the poker game upstairs
> broke up under duress
> and the man who fled with the pot
> found a vacant bed somewhere
> burrowed in
> and slept . . .

> days the ranchers and their hands
> pushed selling stock into the pens
> to ship away for summer wages
> and the bar roared day and night
> until the ranches called them back
> broke and heavy-headed . . .

Everything around you speaks cattle
and each newly tapped keg of beer
bellows like a spring-crazed steer
and it isn't hard to imagine . . .

> nights and days of cowpokes
> sucking brown bottles of Calgary or Pil
> swapping present, past and future
> never more than an arm's length
> from a hind-quarter of beef

And the Winchester '73 mounted on the wall
is a constant reminder to remove your hat.

The Windsor Hotel, Buchanan

Two farmers sit at separate tables
                    in silence
their backs to one another
the only patrons of the moment.

The question of an irrigation ditch
                    divides them
and has for ten silent years
of back-to-back neglect.

Their harvest — grain and children
                    grown and gone
wheat and barley, sons and daughters
grown and gone, east and west.

Soon they will have only
each other and the silence.

Booba

They say he was struck by lightning
as a child, but no one seems to know
whether this is just a bit of legendry
or whether he was born speechless
a shambling bear who has always
tottered from table to table
mouthing meaningless sounds
winning beer and favour
with his perpetual smile.

The man who sits alone in the corner
they say is Booba's brother
though no one has ever seen them
share a beer, or even a sign.

Booba sits for the moment, quiet
shaking only slightly as he sips
quivering like a dog anticipating
his master's slow caress, ignored
except for the casual
glances of his tablemates who are
warmed by a dark irony.

Borden Hotel

The white-haired man bent behind his Pilsener
can even remember the building of this hotel:

> 1906 it was, he says
> Radisson's wasn't built
> till the following year, he adds
> with obvious satisfaction.

He also remembers that this old frame hotel
had a long hardwood bar with a brass footrail
and that you could buy any kind of drink
(that is, until the drought of prohibition).

> 1914 it was, he says
> closed the bars down tight
> until '37, then they decided
> beer parlours were all right
> for men at least, he says.

He tells us how he approved the changes made
allowing women into the premises now so that
the men didn't come in leaving their women
out in the car in the cold with the kids.

> 1969 it was, he says
> Borden always voted it down
> but Radisson voted it in.
> The fellows here took their women
> over there on a Saturday night
> and Borden was left a ghost town.

The pubkeeper joins the old fellow and us
and argues that the trouble with talking
to guys as old as this local history text
is that none of us can possibly question
the authenticity of the old man's memory.

Hell, he says, for all we know
he might be making it all up.

Beginnings

1.

In the beginning there was
always the wind

wind and the sound.

2.

Wind and sun
hammer verbs
into the brain.

Later you learn
the language,
frost, blackening
leaves of summer,

the sounds,
spring's entrance
dropping slowly
from the eaves,

in the night
the call, the geese
flowing overhead
against stars.

3.

Around the quarter-section
barbed wire loops and sags
from rotting willow posts
mauled into the stubborn earth
by sledge and sweat.

Now, long after
the cattle have been sold
white-tailed deer pause
gather limbs to leap
over the wire strands.

4.

The poem is not
the rusted knots
that bind the prairie mind:

it is a sharp-tailed grouse
the sole reminder
an impaled wing
that flaps now on the wire
like some unremembered
signal.

5.

Thorns are words
in the buckbrush
of the dark coulee;
they slash the tongue
rip away the softness
in the light of autumn.

Ancestral Dance

The violin my grandfather
staunchly called a fiddle
but refused to play for us
held for him some magic link
with the man he was.

Left at home alone when we
were safely distant for the day
he'd uncase the fiddle,
rosin the bow with trembling fingers.

Caught in the mystery of the past
he delayed death, bowed the fragments
of a life that was always private,
even on a crowded dancefloor.

In the gathering silence
of seventy years
with fumbling recall he
became the dance.

Burning Tumbleweeds

When we were kids, my brother an' me,
my dad was crippled and couldn't get around much,
so he taught us how to spear tumbleweeds
on the tines of the pitchfork,
stack 'em in piles on the field
until we had many tumbleweed mounds
ready to be set afire and burned away
(Dad used to call it hellfire
burnin' up sinners).

He'd light a match, set ablaze
a dried tumbleweed on my pitchfork
an' I'd run from one pile to another
turnin' each pile into a bonfire.

Then one morning we was burnin'
tumbleweeds stacked the day before.
The first pile burst into flames
an' a rabbit came outta that pile,
fur burnin' an' smellin' awful,
an' I knew there was others
still trapped in that tumbleweed fire,
burnin' up like weeds.

The squealin' of them rabbits
dyin' in there, trapped in that damn fire . . .
I never burned another tumbleweed.
Even now I can't stand the sight of one.
I never thought I could hate a weed so much
but I guess there's more to it than that.

Frost Warning

Last night we argued
over whether to cover the garden —
protect the delicate tomatoes,
the fragile cucumber vines,
whether the bruising of tender plants
caused by discarded sheets and clothes
was worth the effort, knowing
early frost was a slim risk.

But you are a practical woman,
not given to gambles,
and I am the poker player.

We compromised as usual:
you went out and covered the plants.

It didn't freeze and this morning
we are both happy, both winners.
I guess that's how it's always been.

Reflection

Today my grandfather's bones ache.
My father's back is stiff.
And the ghosts of both
look back at me
while I shave.

Homestead

1903. Ride the CPR to Yorkton, end of the line.
The Doukhobors are already there. Four years.
Walk north by west. Buy wagons, horses, grandfather.
(If you can. They're going fast. The price is climbing.)
Move to the land, northwest to Buchanan —
unknown name in an unknown land,
past Good Spirit Lake, twelve miles of water.
Camp on the sand dunes and rest a while.

Claim the land, build the log shack chinked with mud.
Hew the poplar stands, the willow thickets,
hazel nut, saskatoons, chokecherry bushes.
Hone the axe's edge, grandfather,
the land must be cleared for wheat and oats.
Grub out the stubborn roots.
Trim the straightest trees for the buildings
for many are needed — a barn, the house,
the sheds to come. And firewood, grandfather,
you have heard stories about the winters.
Stack the deadfall in piles for sawing later.
Sharpen the axe again. Keep chopping.
Summer is fast fading, grandfather.
This morning the water pail was filmed with ice
and the axe rang like a yodel down a fiord.
Keep chopping, grandfather. Winter is coming
and the prairie wind breathes frost.

Old Injuries

The aroused dog struts
stiff-legged and militant,
paws the grass four-footed,
hurling behind him green blades
and a spatter of pebbles.

The neighbour's team and wagon
is still half a mile away
but something
swells in the dog's throat
raises each hair along his back,
calls forth some old injury
against this one man
who lives inside the dog
like a wound.

Métis Rifle Pits at Batoche

Sure I've seen d'rifle pits of d'Mehtees.
After all I've lived here all my life
and my fadder showed me lotsa dem
before dey got ploughed under and overgrown.

Where? Well you see dat clumpa chokecherry
over dere, maybe quarter-mile or so sout'west?
If you walk over dere to dat clumpa bushes
you'll find d'rifle pit dat ain't been touched.

Nobody ever bodders walkin' into dat bush
and even if dey did dey prob'ly wouldn' know
what d'slight hole in dere is anyhow.
I've seen it many times since I was a kid.

Why not? Well nobody ever asked me before
and dere ain't many people int'rested anyway.
Dem dat does come round always lets on
dey know all about it — so I don't say much.

44

The Ravens

After the dust had finally settled,
after Middleton's victorious militia
had quitted their zareba near Batoche,
taking with them what they had brought,
all they had plundered, and Riel besides,

two black-garbed sisters from Batoche
flapped about the empty encampment,
alert eyes probing the trenches,
darting through the trampled grasses
as they scavenged for left-overs,

seizing a cast-iron pot, an old tea kettle,
a cheap tin fork, discarded or forgotten,
a battered cup whose owner no longer needed
the early morning chill dispelled with tea,
removed forever from military routine
by a shot from Gabriel Dumont's rifle.

Epithalamion

Inside the door the wedding party
commandeers gifts, each in turn
added to the tissue paper pyramid.
Handshakes, quick forehead pecks
and down the receiving line
to the keeper of the teapot
shot glass in hand, line's end,
the ritual act to seal the welcome:
ounce-and-a-half of home brew
snapped back, swallowed, internal blast,
almost-tears, paralyzed voice —
then the welcome is behind
and another dancer takes his place.

Squat, rough-fingered, the fiddler
thrusts his rosined bow over the strings.
His fiddle leaps, springs like a Cossack mare.
He rides the wild tune across distant steppes
like his father and grandfather before him:
the blood of his ancestors rings in the strings.
He turns the darkness of wet spring night
into a happy madness of stamping feet
where colors blur and bodies whirl.

The bride's father, face ruddied with brew
and the wild spinning kolomeykas,
smiles at the new pair, now safe
with each other, the moment theirs
as they turn slow circles on the floor,
the hub of the wheel of clapping guests.

And onstage the old man plays on,
his bow rising and plunging
through centuries, across oceans
in his command of the night.

Water Skier

Evening on Greig Lake
is a sudden shattered sunburst.

The water skier — sorcerer
peels a layer of glass
and hurls it at the dropping sun.

Retirement

And so, old friend, you slap the chalk dust off
clap your hands together with finality
turn in your last set of marks with glee
and storm into superannuation,
retirement gift in hand.
But the chalk dust of the classroom
will not leave you, nor would we want
to see you change your new life.
Rather, be like Emily Carr
in her final bed-ridden years:

presented with her Governor-General's medal
for *Klee Wyck,* she bit the medal
and with disdain declared
that it wasn't real bronze,
then said to the woman
who had brought her the medal,

"There's a dead sparrow
in the eavestrough outside.
Now you take that medal
and beat it against the eaves
until that sparrow falls out —
that's all that damn thing
is good for anyway."

The Wedge

Like the wedge that cleaves the seed
into unborn halves
the memory of you
is angry wind in cat-tails,
the ragged wound you scored
with words opens again
and my cry is the plant
that will not grow.

I am an empty packet
staked in the rows of your plot,
jabbed to earth in anger
like the wedge that cleaves the seed.

Shitepoke

shikepoke / sloughpump
shike/poke   slough/pump
shitepoke   shitpoke
what does it matter now?

> shikepoke or sloughpump
> the memory fades   fades
> we name and then unname
> but it was our word   good enough
> for anyone but ornithologists
> who latinize the bird world

the plains Cree named it
moo-ku-hoo-sew
naming the evening sound
when an Indian says the name
you can smell summer slough

and the first French trader
named it *butor*   then plunged
his paddle deep to pass by

> does it really matter
> that this bird
> is really the *yellow bittern*
> (though no one I know
> ever heard or used this name)?

we didn't know that shitepoke
was some English settler's way
of naming the bird
that shits when it leaps
to flight from the slough

I can still hear
the pump-handle sound cut the evening
still mould in my throat
the shitepoke sound

shikepoke / sloughpump
you are my language   my image
shike/poke   slough/pump

Hawk/Trout

A hawk is a kite
that no string holds
a trout that no line
bends to its will.

A hawk circles
deliberate, patient
before plunging
into blood.

A trout reads surfaces
rises in silence
snaps its jaws, swirls
and is gone.

Spring Snow

Morning breaks cold, slumps
like a slicker on the black spruce.
Grey sky mutes the early light.

We rise from warm beds to fish
and through the cabin windows
watch the first drift and sift of flakes.

Against the dark spruce white
flakes, cotton patches parachute
soundless to the needled earth.

This unwanted intrusion of winter
numbs, draws us from the window
to enclose each other in our warmth.

Then the snow ceases, silent
as its beginnings. The ground betrays nothing.
We open the door to spring and fish.

Samaritans on the Hanson Lake Road

The car crouches motionless on the approach.
It is past midnight. A figure
on the roadside beckons us; we stop.
The Woods Cree tells us his battery
is dead and he can't start the car
without a push. The silent Ford
has two windows boarded with plywood.
We pile out, all six of us
and the avalanche catches him off-guard.
At his suggestion we push
the car backwards, roll it
slowly, then pick up speed.
He throws the clutch,
the engine engages with a roar
and he fishtails wildly backwards
in a spray of gravel, a spatter
against the forest darkness.
He slams the brakes, guns
the motor, rockets ahead
while we leap and scatter
from his single-mindedness.
A terse blare of horn
and he is gone. We watch
his tail-lights fade
like tiny red fireflies
until darkness takes over again.

Jan Lake

George, our silent Cree guide
cuts the outboard motor
as we troll slowly past a rocky point,
wordlessly allows the boat
to drift towards the shoreline.
I think:
George is hungry, so it's lunchtime.
George thinks it's time to stretch our legs.
George needs to take a piss.

We drift towards a clump of willows
jutting like an afterthought from the rock
and George seems intent on something.
I look eagerly, but see nothing at all.
The boat touches the rocks of the point
and at last we see the three large eggs
camouflaged in their feathery nest.
We stare in silence.

Loon, George says softly
and starts the motor again.

Matins

The lake lies before us, winter's reverie
where distant shorelines are fringes of waking.

Our boat skims over unseen life below
to pools where dreams and fish run deep.

I trail my hand in the passing water's cold,
feel the numbness like cold day breaking.

Dreams are fish that swim through our nights,
cold ghosts that swirl throughout our winter sleep.

First Fish

The assembly of rod and reel:

bolt the reel into place,
run line through the eyes
of the rod, knot the leader
to unyielding snugness,
then the walleye jig, a lead head.
The frozen minnow impaled
on the single barbed hook.

The first deliberate cast.

The slow sinking of the line,
quelling the impatience, the desire
to rush the lure back to the boat,
the silent counting before the retrieve.
The jerky retrieval of the lure,
picturing the minnow on the bottom
darting forward in quicksilver flashes.

Waiting for the moment, waiting
for the sudden lurch of the rod,
the arcing fibreglass,
the tremor that vibrates
from fingers to shoulders.

Waiting for the first fish.
Waiting for the memory,
the reawakening.

Knives and Fish

The old Swampy Cree in the filleting shed
watches our slow butchery of fish
and finally says to us,
Here, I show you howta fillet
d'walleye, dere's nuttin to it atall.

He grasps a plump walleye by the head
pulls a filleting knife from its sheath
makes several quick passes behind the gills
slashes the belly open, slices the side
strips back one side of fish from head to tail
in a flash of fillet, flips the fish over
and flakes the other fillet.

Knives and fish hold no secrets for him.

But we, mouths agape like pike-strikes,
disbelievers at an illusionist's show
stare, try to peel away some small deceit,
something that will explain it all.

See dese bones here? Watch.

He flips the fillet meat-side down
places his thumb on the scales above the bones
slides his knife under the fillet
along the filleting table under the pressure
of his thumb with a soft snick
lifts the fillet, shows us the bones,
a neat sliver lying on the table.

Y'see. Nuttin to it.
Now you do it.

He grins and walks away
wiping his knife blade on his jeans.

Reefs

Below placid surfaces lie
fists of rock. Unseen

they wait like anger, quick
to destroy the rash.

Indian guides have learned
avoidance of these reefs. We

name this history. We try
to fathom their internal maps,

but like our words, our vision
fails us here.

Fish Inspectors

The walleye fishing has been spectacular.
We have limited out our three boats
in an hour or so — eight fish apiece.
Arthur Custer has counted the fish like beads
and knows: each boat has the exact number allowed.
Nothing here will jeopardize his guiding licence.
He explains that the new game wardens
on Jan are *real mean bastards*.

On our return to camp a boat hails us.
Two wardens pull us alongside for inspection.
They collect our licences, note details,
count each boat's catch with the slow scrutiny
of electoral officers in a recount.

Custer sits impassive through it all,
until one officer turns to him and says,
"Pretty good fishing for so short a time.
Where'd you catch them all, Arthur?"

Arthur wears his disdain like mesh.
His face permits only a trace
of trickster impishness as he replies,
"On the lake."

Fallen on Hard Times

It has been two years
since we last saw our guide.
His face has aged ten years,
his paunch, grown vaster now,
slumps over his jeans
as he limps past our doorway.
We invite him in for morning coffee.

He tells us how he broke
his ankle in three places last winter
falling down some steps. Barred
from the pub along with his son,
they have both been relegated
to the filleting shed with the women.

But he voices no complaints,
harbours no grudges we can feel,
just bears this toll of shame
in silence, serves his time.

Shuffleboard Magician

Wagner is totally hooked on fish tales
played out like line between Blues and Pils,
when this Indian shuffleboard player
at the board just behind our table
walks up behind Wagner, leans over
his right shoulder, and slips
his hand into Wagner's jacket pocket.
The table locks in sudden silence.

The Indian says nothing, just fumbles
in Wagner's pocket. I am wondering:
How will Wagner play this?
when the Indian draws back his hand,
flashes us all a winning grin
and a shuffleboard rock that has
somehow landed in Wagner's pocket,
then walks away to his game.

On the Pooltable

Penner and I have our challenge on the board:
we are eager to unseat young Brian from the table.
Easily the premier shooter in the bar tonight
he has held the table now for several hours.
Even a succession of weak partners hasn't fazed him.
He holds onto the game and its winnings.
His shirt pocket bulges with a wad of bills, mostly ones,
a few fives, and a ten, beaten from his fellow Crees.

Finally it's our turn. We start badly, botch shots.
It looks like another easy game for Brian,
but we recover and turn the game tight.
At last only two balls are left. Our ten and the eight.
It's my cue. Two easy shots to make for game.
I sink the balls. Brian pays us off and we invite him
to join our table for a beer on us. He is pleased.
We swap stories while we beat back new challengers.

Penner is talking to Brian and I am on the cue.
As I chalk the tip a young Cree woman calls me.
I walk to where she sits alone, bend to her.
You shouldn'ta beat Brian, you know, her voice soft.
He need the money. He just lost his job, you know.
He got no money and he playin' pool for food.
You shouldn'ta beat him. I nod and set to shoot.
But she has beaten me. I miss the shot, lose the game.

It is too late tonight to do Brian any good.
Again I learn that the game here is different.
The rules of pool are always secondary
to the unwritten code of dignity and survival.

Number One Guide

(for John Seewup)

1.

Fifty-six years he has beaten
a life from these dark woods
with a Harper's Island trapline.
And fifty-six summers here
on Jan as boy and man,
            fisherman and guide.

"I'm number one guide,"
                  John shouts.
And who can question this?
He has forgotten more about this lake
than any *moonie-ass* can dream
or ever hope to learn.

But years of booze have bent John
like a rough wind. Lodge owners
hire him now only
                as a last resort.

2.

Forest fires have swept
the camp of all Indian guides, all
but John, here, with the women
and children. His age and condition
a comfortable reprieve
from days and nights of smoke
and heat, and endless shovels.

64

So John is Jan's sole guide:
transformed from last year's pariah
to this year's savior, besieged
with requests and promises.
American twenties and bottles
of Old Crow swirl around him
like the dangerous drift of smoke.

3.

In the morning the camp rises
on Seewup time and John heads
his flotilla of American boats
strung behind like empty promises
to Deschambault River.
                              We decline
his offer to follow him,
                              prefer
to map-read our own route
alone to Grassy Narrows where
we will find other walleyes.
John throws us a jaunty wave
and captains his armada away.

4.

Early afternoon. We have returned
with our limits of walleyes.
John returns with seven boats,
all babbling about *grayet nathren piehk.*

John has been liberally plied with booze.
He has little desire to fillet fish,
looks instead for a beer or whiskey.

He tells us of last winter. Falling
through the ice. His narrow escape.
How his son caught him by the hair,
somehow managed to pull him out.

"By the hair!" he roars, running
his hand through his dark hair.
"John was THAT close!" he shouts.

5.

We show John our map. Where
we have fished. The spot at the Narrows.
Mark it as closely as possible,
indicate where we caught our limits.
John grins. Nods his approval.
But our black X seems to stir something.
He grabs the pen.
                              "Look. I show you!
Best walleye spot.
P.P. Walleye. Look here.
This one right here . . ."

He X's a point on our map.
". . . my favorite. P.P. Walleye."
The X is just off Harper's Island.
His winter grounds.
                              "Here's another.
And this one too."

There are now four X's.

His excitement dies. He stares,
seems embarrassed at his marks.
Finally, *"Don't tell nobody."*
A sadness has taken over.
"You go there. But don't tell
nobody I showed you."
                              Subdued,
he wanders away to his camp,
away from something he understands
and would rather forget. Somehow.

Vespers

Against the fade of light
the spruce line
the lake with dark.

Spectral birch slink
into boreal night
and spruce reach
their ragged arms
to bring down the light.

One Man

The easy laughter is gone now.
Face pinched, a darkness has settled
for John. Last year his son. Dead,
victim of another's jealousy, cut
down by a shotgun blast at a party.
A few days ago, his sister,
one who was closest, gone.
John wears his grief in his eyes
as long as he can. Then breaks
as we all must. As we must
wear his grief with us
this night, and tomorrow,
carry it away when we leave.
There is no other way.

Sunday Leaving

Once again we are leaving.
The weekend catch of walleyes safely stowed,
ready for the long ride back.
We pack our gear.
An hour ago we said goodbye.
Arthur Custer's final words:
   I'll see you next year, maybe
   if I'm still alive.

A darkness etched on the hour.
Saskatoon. We will pick up our lives
in that world. One last look
around the camp — the white cabins and the dark
trees, sun-glint on the lake, Arthur Custer,
home.

The Return

The song of return
is not the song of journeys out.

We are tired, our faces burn
with unaccustomed wind and sun.

Fish fade from our minds.
The talk is low, desultory.

Long silences settle and bind,
a closeness comfortable as praise.

In hours we will be back within the maze,
our other lives.   Another spring, and north.

Saskatchewan Town at Night

Thirty-seven thousand feet below me
the town barely exists. And yet
somewhere in that faint scatter of lights
a woman has just walked out behind her house,
worn by her day with kids. She stops on the patio,
lights a cigarette, flips the spent match
into the dark, looks up to the stars
and there I am, five miles above her eyes

curious traveller, stranger who might
have been lover, part of this bond
of just-visible lights: she,
drawn for a moment to this moving star,
transported to her most intimate fantasy;
me, reaching down to touch,
touch with words the darkness,
her night, this small moment.

Alexandra

Twenty years forgetting can
never wipe our memories clean.

Newpapers forget. Telecasts can
not outlive each day's new killings.

The beauty contest you won is forgotten.
The patients you nursed are well, or dead.

The river grasses no longer hear
the screaming in your blood.

The police have found new mysteries,
new bloodlettings, new victims.

But somewhere a tormented man
sits in darkness of his own,

and no river can wash from his mind
the slow flow of your dying.

He can not twist his hands enough
to wipe the feel of your flesh away.

Each day your face will grow
younger in his album of dark recall

until the day he will believe
it love and must tell all.

Cold Bus Ride

We ride the bus together
                this cold January morning,
clothed heavily in silence,
                strangers sharing a seat,
each of us benumbed
                by bitter wind,
reluctant and withdrawn,
                no desire to speak,
or even force a smile
                in our seclusion.
We are private and defensive,
                our need for words
frozen, left behind
                at wind-torn bus stops.

Only when our bus halts
                and we both must rise
from the same seat do we
                smile at each other,
tentative acknowledgement
                that we have shared
fifteen minutes of our lives
                close to one another
sharing nothing more
                than body warmth.

Hope to Princeton

Hope wears a shroud,
fog and sporadic drizzle,
as I ascend the twisted road,
my headlights a vain thrust
against dawn's greyness,
up across Hope slide —
the massive rockface
that tumbled down, making
this new highway, still inching
against the mountain, mute
several years later.

Up the rough road I creep,
clinging to the tail-lights
of the car ahead:
tiny twin nerves
red beacons pulsing
in the near obscurity.

Finally, the heights.
I break free of fog,
break into a blue brilliance,
light that cascades down
slopes with sudden fire,
fuses feather-gold larches
to sombre firs and pines,
a startle of colour
giddies and catapults
the spirits as the road
unbends and levels
into the primal wonder
of Manning Forest.

Hippos and Bikers

Radium Hot Springs this August afternoon
is as any other mountain day
a congestion of tourists that ring
the hot springs in a drove. Pale hippos
sans mud, half-submerged they bask,
lured to this concrete wallow, pilgrims
multi-coloured in bikinis and trunks
luxuriating hip to hip around the pool.

Inside the National Hotel just down the road
cold beer is swirled in glasses as the locals
counter summer's heat with beaded bottles,
fine brews from Creston: Kokanees and Kootenays,
and amber bubbles rise to snowy heads.
Here, apart from the hippo hive we stop,
my wife and I, freed from the wheel and drive,
content to let cold beer bring down the sun.
The rumble of low talk and clink
of bottle against glass encloses us.

The door yanks someone from the sun and heat.
Black-leathered biker, helmet in hand,
wind-strewn hair akimbo, steps inside,
a second, third and fourth clone hard on heels.
The door has barely snubbed the sun again
when one more group of four or five clump through,
a militant percussion of heavy boots.
Each one is bearded, pony-tailed, or hair askew,
each black-leathered back speaks
in artless craft of Reapers and Chiefs,
Rebels and Kings from cities of the west.
The door swings open and shut, open and shut,
the march of helmets and jackets grows.
The throng musters at the back of the pub
and beer flows down to meet the thirst.

75

The last one is finally seated in the pub.
Two bikers commandeer a window at the front,
survey the street outside, the bike pack
now at rest in silence, chrome aglint.
There are at least forty-five bikes out there,
my wife announces softly. That's too much
for several tables in this sudden power shift.
Beers are drunk in haste, tables empty:
they know wild tales of bike gang terror.
Outside the hotel six bikers are deployed,
late afternoon sentries for the bikes.

Several bikers stroll from table to table,
exchange unheard remarks with others.
Some wear headbands, some neckerchiefs, most
wear greasy jeans, almost all over thirty.
The room wears their presence in quiet.
A smell of fear hangs in the heavy smoke.

Across the street a single cop arrives,
sits in his car in the service station lot,
feigns casual talk to passersby, pretends
he does not see across the street
this gleaming invasion of spoke and chrome.
Minutes slide away like good draught beer.
The pub, its tables now all taken, drinks
in strange solemnity, all conversation
the low drone of prayer — no guffaws
or high whinnies, no bellows or gut-shakers,
nothing to impart the normal to the place.
And the bikers have established the tone,
their air of propriety has deceived us all.

Inside an hour they rise as one and leave,
a barrage of heavy heels, and as they pass
I notice knives in sheaths slung from belts
that slap against their thighs as they retreat.
One by one the motors catch and growl, the roar
of Harley, Yamaha, Suzuki shakes mountain air.
Helmets snap in place as one by one they roll
away to shatter evening. The mountie disappears.
The young bartender pastes his smile in place
and moves among the tables to gather glasses.

Fish Creek

A grassy riverbank clearing near Fish Creek.
Here Middleton was humbled by Dumont,
some Metis sharpshooters and a few Indians.
A small gravesite, staked with metal palings.
A solitary monument remembers the militia,
the deaths of Middleton's men.
There is no mention of other deaths.
No suggestion of defeat of a superior force
by a raggle-taggle band of illiterates.

But almost a hundred years later this site
still embarrasses, rankles like an old wound —
a little-used dirt trail, lack of road signs.

A few miles downriver towards Batoche
the spire of the Metis church leans against sky.
In the softness of summer night at Fish Creek
fiddle sound floats on the night wind;
ghosts dance on the banks of the South Saskatchewan.
Sashes flame in the firelight.
There are too many ghosts, their graveyard
too large to hide.

The History of China
(for Andy & Patrick)

Backwards 7000 years in Chinese history,
through a maze of ancient wisdom, backwards
in time so remote and distant
there can be no focus on friends,
three poets in a country
where history is a story of grandfathers
and seventy centuries lies beyond
the boundaries of our minds.

My friends are caught in a frenzy of images:
they are writing poems about China.
One has visited the country and roots
poems in the fertile soil of touch and dream,
a landscape he may never see again
except as ragged moths of memory drawn
against the windows, against the night.
The other moves through remembered pages
read of Chinese sailors, emigrants who left
precarious certainties of home to seek
unknown familiarities of distant shores.
The eyes of my friends are pools of vigilance
where strange fish swin, delicate as silk
stitched into the fragile embroidery of remembrance.

And I am the curious third of this tentative bond,
one who shambles through the silences of the others
who are so intent to draw to them the voices,
fragments that may speak to them today, somewhere
down this promenade of Oriental time. Perhaps
these antique voices that sing in their ears
may have some least words to whisper to me.

Ontario Museum of Science
Toronto, May 1982

79

Wood Mountain October

Subtleness of October sun. Coulees aflame.
Wind smells winter. Trees draw into themselves.

Three mule deer. Against a fading hillside.
A ring of stones. Forgotten stories.

This empty homestead. A lone spruce.
Memories in other minds, distant places.

Sun slant on stubble. Harvest aftermath.
Mallards feeding, heads green as spring.

Geese. Etched lines on sky. Autumn's cliché.
Cock pheasant on the road. Brilliant arrogance.

The beauty in this land. Summer's death.
We believe in this. The wonder of the seed.

Eating in Sault Ste. Marie

The bread was otherwise excellent:
warm, crusty, fresh.
As the knife sawed the loaf
the slice that fell aside
revealed the fly.

It wasn't that the fly
was doing anything obnoxious.
On the contrary, it was
motionless, as flies seldom are.
But it had somehow committed
the tactical (and fatal) error,
landing on the bread dough
at the inopportune moment.
The kneading entombed it.

I hold no grudge against the fly:
we all make our own blunders.
Yet because the knife
has brought its presence to light
the waiter must be summoned,
the salad checked for crawling things.
It can not be ignored.

Hamburgers and Beer
(for Tom and Perry)

Vancouver sprawls, a lounging teen
on the Fraser delta couch, feet elevated
on the arm of the mountains, head
lolling in the sand. We are sitting
sipping beer, munching burgers outdoors
when the first siren wails up 4th.
It lends incongruous punctuation
to our talk of poetry. The flashing red,
the raucous passing prompt silence.
There is nothing unusual in this.
No poem here to startle the moment.
We are ready to resume earnest words,
perhaps probe a few cracks in the universe.
Now a second siren grows on the dying
of the first: another cherry-blinking car
roars past, a motorcycle cop in pursuit. Now
the scene begins to feel like a poem.
We sit at this sidewalk table, spectators.
Someone's real-life drama impinges,
somewhere near, someone's story unfolds.

A poem is growing and we are all a part of it.
We all have some of the same lines, but now
we must fill the gaps, find beginnings, endings.
Must be a bad accident at an intersection,
says one. *Looks serious,* adds another. No need
to mention the given lines. Now we are given
more — two more patrol cars scream past.
The poem now veers in another direction.
Could be a bank hold-up. Maybe a murder.
No one says it, but now we anticipate,
wait for the next signal — ambulance.
Right on cue it speeds onto the scene,
flashes by with a roar and a wail.
Should be on the supper news at 6:00,
someone says. It might have been me.

Poems are accumulations of images, remembered
or imagined. Some may be real. I
think we resumed our talk of poetry and people
and dreams. Or we may all have been writing
the poem in our heads, seeking the key
to release the spill of language,
to make it our own. Poems write themselves
every day in this city. Everywhere
around us people read the words
etched on the city's movement.

The Hookers of St. John's

Below street level in the Seabreeze lounge
seamen reel in from the world's boats,
fishermen cast up from western Europe,
from Asia and from South America,
their ships at anchor a block or so away.

Inside the Seabreeze several idle whores
exchange tidbits about the latest ship.
Hookers like gulls await each new crew,
their lines ready for sea-weary men.
They ply their nets in every language,
in wordless language, unwritten messages
to men who need women. They are universal,
these fishers of the Seabreeze,
part of the city like the gulls.
They cry out their welcome, cast out lines
to each new ship. Their perfume rides
the waves of cigarette smoke, the harbour smell.

Pouch Cove

North of St. John's
fishermen unload their boats
in this tiny rock-squeezed cove,
signal to the fish shack perched
above them, a seabird on the rock.
A bucket of fish creaks
up tired pulleys to the shack.

In the fish shed others gut,
split and clean the catch.
Fish waste plummets down troughs,
splatters on rocks, or tumbles
into the salt chuck for scavengers.
Frenzied gulls wheel and scream,
fishing boats come, one by one.

One fisherman hauls his boat ashore
up a forty-five degree ramp of planks,
cajoled by a cranky engine that sputters
at its pulleys and cables.
Another fork-loads a last bucket,
while a third manoeuvers his dory
into the cove with his catch.

On this coast where sea meets rock
men grow roots on the tenuous shore,
bob like glass floats
on an uncertain sea.

Pouch Cove, Nfld. 1978

The Streets of Tijuana

1.

The Indian woman, a squat dark lump
less than five feet tall. Strapped
to her back an infant son sleeps.
She accosts tourists one by one
with cheap pendants, brooches.
Her brown eyes are pools. Grief,
where no fish leap or splash.
She thrusts her hand, her baubles
at Sunday border-crossing gringos.
Her child sleeps, ignorant of his fate —
to scrabble these dirty streets
for American dollars.

2.

This Indian boy may be five years old,
candidate for kindergarten elsewhere.
A hummingbird, he darts back and forth
flitting in the sidewalk throng.
His would-be play is serious:
he carries a carton of Wrigley's gum,
sells it by the pack to the tourists.

3.

The smell of burritos. A street vendor
at the corner hawks his spicy food.
*Whatever you do in Tijuana, do not
eat the food or drink the water!*
Nearby a burro harnessed to a cart.
You may sit in the cart for a fee,
not to ride, but to pose for photos.

4.

Shopkeepers cajole and wheedle,
lure strollers into the grubby dimness,
barter American dollars for leather purses,
woollen serapes, sheepskin vests and sombreros,
jewelry, cheap watches, glassware and tequila.
Sleek and well-fed, Tijuana merchants
banter ageless ploys, nose-to-nose.
Their lines are well-rehearsed.
Their share of tourist dollars will be counted
on the mongering skills of their tongues.

5.

Taxis shudder on Tijuana streets.
Their sole function the transport of tourists
from the border just a mile away.
From the border taxi compound the rate is fixed,
but the return demands haggling with the driver.
American cab fleet rejects, these taxis
are cacophonies of rattles, squeaks and groans.
They jounce and lurch from pothole to cobble.

6.

At the border the taxi slows,
shudders to a wheezing stop,
releases the departing tourists.
Four small boys leap and scramble
to be first to the cab's back doors,
first to yank open the door and stand
expectant, upturned palm extended:
one last clutch for unspent gringo dollars.

Goldfish and Bumblebees

Sitting at a little table
in this hometown restaurant,
confident in his territory, the poet
chooses his poems from early work,
opens his world to us here.

Sometimes he is the goldfish
and we, gawkers, peer through the glass.
Yet the image is clear
as the water he glides through,
swims through with natural ease.

Sometimes he is the bumblebee,
wrapped in the flower's close,
locked into love's last bloom
as winter stills the world of bees.
Yet song transcends the season.

His singing swims and buzzes
over and around and through
us all, murmurs of Dickinson
and McEwen, Pound and Yeats
and other singers locked in his tongue.

Closer and closer we are drawn
into a nectared world of words,
sounds that flash and flutter
through the glass and petals of poems
to pull around us walls of art.

Tough Vernal Sentiments

Driving to Esterhazy on this last day
in March I have passed from spring
showers to sunshine,
and now near Lanigan the old
seasonal struggle comes skidding into focus.
I am caught in a prairie blizzard,
fighting snow driven by a northwest wind,
steering with two-handed tentativeness
on this treacherous highway to spring.

And through the slanting snow
just above the road ahead I see
two Canada geese struggle, ragged
against the bite of wind.
Their plaintive cries carry
the breath of spring,
push dogged winter north.

Rituals

It was a beat-up blue '46 Chevy,
92,000 miles on the odometer,
tires that couldn't withstand a vicious mosquito,
a radiator that leaked and over-heated,
a manual transmission that locked at stoplights
or whenever the perversion seized it,
a trunk lid that wouldn't close
and a front door that wouldn't open,
a flat six engine that did credit
to any six somnambulant dray horses.
But it was my first car:
such minor deficiencies were unimportant.

It knocked and clattered me over dusty roads,
was unfailing to start, never quit on me —
its only perversity to clench its gears
against walls or angle-parked to a curb
and especially at stoplights in rush hour.
I learned to leap from behind the wheel,
sprint to the front, spring the hood,
and flip the stubborn gear in place.

One Saturday night on the way to a wedding dance
it turned over its hundred thousandth mile.
The occasion demanded its moment of respect,
an impressive string of zeros on the odometer.
So we stopped there on that country road,
brought the world to a complete standstill
while the old Chevy rested, maybe dreamed
of rolling off the assembly line in 1946.
We knew nothing of rituals then,
but sensed the history of the moment,
knew some special ceremony was demanded.

We unfolded our gangling legs from the Chev,
dispersed ourselves, fore and aft,
and each of us pissed against a tire.
We gave her fenders a congratulatory thump,
each offered up a witty note of praise,
then climbed back in and rolled away.

So why do I recall it all now?
Me, despiser of so many pseudo-rites and ceremonies,
one for whom tribal eating is sheer torment?
Maybe it was the total spontaneity:
not that we *had* to do it, but that we *wanted* to;
not that we understood, but wanted understanding.

Morning of Hoar Frost

This morning hoar frost
rims the outer world, trees
rimed, cold beauty.

A few leaves still
tremble in their dance
on the pale Griffin poplar.

This backyard world once more
a snapshot of the past,
a reminder of other frost:

the child I was, city-born,
learning winter in Saskatchewan
at ten on a prairie farm;

this same frost feathered
aspen groves like snow,
and the world was a frozen sea.

My patient uncle explained
the difference between snow
and this lacework of frost.

And now that this same trim
of white has won over my hair
with its own wintry reminder

these fragile frost-work mornings
sing a pale and delicate song.
Time pauses on the edge of rime.

Girl in the Black Lounge Chair

Waiting for my night class to begin,
smoking that one last cigarette,
I notice the girl
curled in the black lounge chair
reading a letter, lost
to everything around her.

Her eyebrows arch suddenly.
Her lips move in silence, break
into a momentary smile, then
she closes the letter slowly,
touches it lightly to her lips,
returns it to the envelope.

For a moment her eyes touch mine.

I go to my class troubled:
a young girl, her smile, a message,
these small moments, so many
letters I should have written.

The Road from Nelson to Vernon

At New Denver the asphalt begins
its tortuous climb. It is a brilliant day,
the mountains buttress a blue sky.

It was all Wayman's idea: Nelson to Vernon
via Nakusp and the Monashee Pass.
An incredible drive! You'll love it.

And it's true. The day defies metaphors
and Sorestad, alone behind the wheel, hums
and twists his yellow Malibu from turn to turn.

He busies himself with mental notes of shapes,
lets colours and contrasts etch freely on his memory,
lets the asphalt wind him up the mountainside.

New Denver. Without warning two lanes end
and one thin string of pavement clings
against this wall of stone, a single trail.

Sorestad wonders whether he has missed a sign,
taken a wrong turn, and now is lost
on some long-neglected one-way logging road.

His agile mind conjures a huge Mack truck
laden with tons of fir logs, chained
to a flatbed, swooping around the next bend,

and he wonders what he can possibly offer
when his Malibu questions the monster Mack
over the right to this single hair of highway.

The results are too unsettling to consider,
so he presses on and up, blots out images
of his Malibu tumbling, tumbling . . .

94

Sorestad drives faster, the Malibu's tires
protest as he wrenches each hairpin; he is
now seized with a single irrational notion:

get up and over this bizarre snake of a road
before some jaded lumber jockey begins descent
from the heights above, looking for easy sport.

Sorestad's eyes are maddened orbs of intent.
He ignores the absence of guard-rails, locked
in fierce passion to this wild twist of road,

he is climbing faster, faster, up and up,
hunched over his wheel, he has blotted everything
from his vision except the road. He is flying

ever upward in a spiral, ascending like smoke,
leaving the car behind entirely, floating free
of the mountain, he has become a golden eagle.

Ah, Wayman, he muses, *so this is the secret!*
He remembers Wayman's smile, Wayman's eyes aglow
just hours before when he recommended the drive.

And Sorestad's Malibu is spiralling ever upward,
teasing the stone-faced mountain, laughing, laughing,
at trucks and cars and campers that creep along . . .

Then it is over. The road becomes two lanes again
and the yellow dividing line reappears. Sorestad
is alone in his Malibu. His hands have become

locks of sinew and bone, his palms are wet.
He is driving into Nakusp enroute to the Monashee.
Sorestad will be in Vernon in another two hours.

Late Night Visit, Humber Valley

On the backyard deck at a friend's in Toronto
I hear the Humber mumble over a weir
down the slope past a tangle of wild grape vines.
I sit and scribble my recollections of the day,
meld impressions and imaginings in my notes.

A strange feeling creeps over me
and I sense the shoe now on the other foot:
the observer now object of silent scrutiny.
My sudden glance freezes the watcher
four feet away on the top step of the deck.
A young raccoon, caught like a thief.
His masked eyes fix me in slow inspection
I return without rancour. Then he retreats,
ambles across the lawn, disappears in the vines,
the maze of wild grapes, the darkness of the valley.

Souster's home is just a few blocks away.
Maybe it's one of his friends, sent round
to offer me a moment's diversion,
a late night welcome to Toronto.

96

Peel & Sherbrooke, Montreal

Desultory rain greys the day.
Umbrellas and raincoats butt
their way to or from destinations,
crabs scuttling sideways in the wind.

On Sherbrooke a city works crew is
ageless and universal in practised lethargy.

At the intersection two white gloves
gesticulate on hidden strings
from beneath the brilliant orange
rain cape of the traffic cop:
a hive of animation against
the methodical leisure of road repairs.

The works crew idle near the corner,
light cigarettes, bandy and ogle
the women who hurry by them.

The white gloves orchestrate the rain
from the orange core of this grey world,
while the road repairs move
in their own slow, timeless rhythm.

Toronto Street Scene

The two of them walk
Yonge Street in rain.
Unhappy pair, her face
wears a mist of hurt;
his is a dark storm.
Step by step they stride
in practised tandem.
Her sorrow tilts an umbrella
over his anger, not as
a shield or a balm,
but because she would
do no less, and he
would do no more.

The Laundromat

See how they measure
their days with detergent and bleach,
quarters for washers and dryers.
Black sacks of clothes, soiled.
They check washers, one by one,
hope to find a clean tub,
at least one that works.

Their clothes at last being washed
they lean back on their bench seats
with magazines and cigarettes.
They slot their time with silence,
pretend others are not there, only
they have sought this time of cleansing.

They rise to empty their washers,
initiate the tumble of dryers.
They watch their days spill
round and round, watch the fabric
reshape itself. Washday depression
loosens as they fold and press
their clean clothes to a neatness
their lives will never have.
The garbage bag of laundry is transformed.
When they leave it is borne
before them, carried with respect.
The clothes assume somehow
the fragility of dreams.

Luther Highrise

Is it only here in Saskatoon
that we thrust the aged upward
like flags in a fit of patriotism,
shoot them up elevator shafts
higher, ever higher,
as if anxious
to get them to their destination
faster, sooner

and how do these veterans of living
feel, cubicled in their concrete
highrise named after a man for whom
faith was everything?
When they enter the elevator
daily for the ride
to the top-floor cafeteria
and someone pushes
that uppermost button,
do they sometimes feel
that this time when they reach
that final floor the elevator
will just continue
to take them
higher?

Beside the Nursing Home

This withered man
has ridden his wheelchair
so long now
there is no longer
envy in his glance,
no expression
as the slim young legs
pass him by.

Cedar Waxwings in January

It's hard to explain:
          suddenly
they're there, that's all —
              the waxwings.
They just appear
          from nowhere
          from a chill blue
or a snow-ripe grey.
              One moment, nothing.
Not a movement
          of any kind
in the whole frozen universe.
              Then,
they're there,
          the waxwings,
winter visitants
          travelling together
          like carollers,
their arrival
          unprompted,
          a gift.
They strip berries
          from alders and cotoneasters,
cluster together
          like schoolchildren.
There is something
          about these birds,
something about
          their manner,
          their jaunty humour,
as they perch together
          to chat
          and nibble.

Certainly it is not
                    the dull grey
of their round bodies,
                    the slatey thrust
of crown, but something
                    about their sudden
presence
          in a frigid landscape,
their arrivals and departures,
and,
      yes,
          the disappointment
their abrupt
          leaving holds
that keeps me
                here, to watch
                in silence,
to write
this poem.

Backyard Moment
(for Ray Souster)

The robin has just settled
into the birdbath and now
cocks its head at me
expectantly.
                Out of habit,
family man that I am,
I turn my eyes away
discreetly.

Autumnal Prelude

This morning the backyard vibrates:
a flash and pipe of unfamiliar birds.
Poplar and cotoneaster tremble
with a host of newcomers
feeding on summer's last insects
or berries of elder and ash.

Other birds clamber the limbs
of silver maple and birch,
pick parasites in the frenzy
of songbirds on migration.

Sojourners only, these birds
are a first reminder, a last
burst of summer, harbingers
of coming cold.

Shelling Peas

In the desert heat of Saskatchewan August
like exhausted dancers peas wilt by mid-day;
you must rise in the early morning to pick
the plump pods at their peak of freshness.

In the shade you sit with three containers:
the basket of peas, waiting to be depearled,
the smaller bucket for the rattle of peas,
the waste container for the emptied pods.
You take care in the placement of the three —
eliminate wasted movement, position each
to suit your handedness, minimize the time
between the plucking of the fresh pod
and expelling of the spent shell.

Your thumbnail becomes an oyster knife
to pry the shell, the thumb slides inside
the violated lips and thrums the gems
into the bucket in a green dance of hail;
the other hand flips the husks away.
In seconds it is a familiar act,
new as spring, ageless as love:
slit of thumbnail, crack of entry,
chorus of peas, snap of discards.
You slip easily into this harvest ritual,
become one with a million others
who ply this same rite of summer.

There is no boredom here in repetition.
Each pod is its own mystery, its own small world.
And you become the eternal peasant, held
in abounding fascination with living things.
You now become a mere extension
of something you sense but can not fully know:
why this ritual courses small, almost imperceptible
tremors through the nerves and sinews of the arm
to warm the thumb and fingers with old messages.
You lapse into the easy movement of the hands
with a satisfaction that lies just below
the skin of consciousness like tiny emeralds
singing their green notes in mid-summer dance.
In the coolness of early morning you turn
the seasons between your thumb and fingers
and hold the rain in your hands.

Books by Glen Sorestad

Jan Lake Poems, Harbour Books, 1984

Ancestral Dances, Thistledown Press, 1979

Pear Seeds in My Mouth, Sesame Press, 1977

Prairie Pub Poems, Thistledown Press, 1976

Windsongs, Thistledown Press, 1975

The THUNDER CREEK CO-OP is a production co-operative registered with the Saskatchewan Department of Co-operatives and Co-operative Development. It was formed to publish prairie writing — poetry, prose, songs and plays.

PUBLICATIONS

HOLD THE RAIN IN YOUR HANDS, a definitive collection of the best from five earlier books, plus new poems by Glen Sorestad, $8.95 pb, $15.95 hc.

TERRITORIES, fresh, distinctive poetry by Elizabeth Allen, $6.00 pb, $14.00 hc.

DOUBLE VISIONS, the first release in the Wood Mountain Series, established to recognize the work of new writers. Poetry by Thelma Poirier and Jean Hillabold, $6.00 pb, $14.00 hc.

KEN MITCHELL COUNTRY, the best of Ken Mitchell, $4.95 pb.

FOREIGNERS, a lively, passionate novel by Barbara Sapergia, $4.95 pb.

MORE SASKATCHEWAN GOLD, exciting, imaginative, masterful short stories from prairie writers, edited by Geoffrey Ursell, $4.95 pb.

HERSTORY 1985, a practical and informative calendar featuring women in Canada, $6.95.

STREET OF DREAMS, poems that recover our lost experiences, our forgotten dreams, by Gary Hyland, $7.00 pb, $15.00 hc.

FISH-HOOKS, thirteen stories from an exciting new talent, Reg Silvester, $6.00 pb, $14.00 hc.

100% CRACKED WHEAT, an excellent source of dietary laughter from Saskatchewan writers, edited by Robert Currie, Gary Hyland and Jim McLean, $4.95 pb.

THE WEATHER, vibrant, marvellous poems by Lorna Crozier, $6.00 pb.

THE BLUE POOLS OF PARADISE, a document of secrets, poems by Mick Burrs, $6.00 pb.

GOING PLACES, poems that take you on a vacation with Don Kerr, $6.00 pb, $14.00 hc.

GRINGO: POEMS AND JOURNALS FROM LATIN AMERICA by Dennis Gruending, $6.00 pb.

NIGHT GAMES, stories by Robert Currie, $7.00 pb.

THE SECRET LIFE OF RAILROADERS, the funniest poems ever to roll down the main line, by Jim McLean, $5.00 pb.

BLACK POWDER: ESTEVAN, 1931, a play with music, by Rex Deverell and Geoffrey Ursell, $5.00 pb.

EARTH DREAMS, startlingly original poems by Jerry Rush, $5.00 pb.

SINCLAIR ROSS: A READER'S GUIDE by Ken Mitchell. With two short stories by Sinclair Ross, $7.00 pb.

SUNDOGS, an anthology of the best in Saskatchewan short stories, edited by Robert Kroetsch, $7.95 pb.

SUPERWHEEL, the musical play about automobiles, with script by Rex Deverell and music and lyrics by Geoffrey Ursell, $5.00 pb.

NUMBER ONE HARD, an L.P. of songs by Geoffrey Ursell from the original Globe Theatre production, "an investigative documentary about the prairie grain industry", $6.00.

EYE OF A STRANGER, poems by Gary Raddysh, $4.00 pb.

ODPOEMS &, poems by E. F. Dyck, $4.00 pb.

All of the above may be ordered from your favourite bookstore or from:

coteau books

THUNDER CREEK CO-OP
Box 239, Sub. #1
Moose Jaw, Saskatchewan
S6H 5V0

DATE DUE
DATE DE RETOUR